Puzzled

Also by Ruth Maus

Valentine: Poems
Meadowlark Press, 2019

Puzzled

Poems by **Ruth Maus**

Art by Katja Weiss

Meadowlark
PRESS
Emporia, Kansas, USA

Meadowlark Press, LLC
meadowlarkpoetrypress.com
P.O. Box 333, Emporia, KS 66801

Puzzled—Copyright © Ruth Maus, 2022

Images by Katja Weiss. Used with permission.

POETRY / Women Authors
POETRY / Subjects & Themes / General
POETRY / American / General

ISBN: 978-1-956578-25-6

Library of Congress Control Number: 2022945261

To the creative spirit in each of us, to the light in every heart.

ABOUT THIS BOOK

As a Kansas poet I'd like to introduce you to Katja Weiss, a German painter and my distant cousin, whom I have never met. In 1882 my antecedent immigrated to the United States from Pomerania (now part of Poland), while Katja's side stayed behind and settled in Germany. Amazingly, both branches remained in touch despite two world wars, different languages, thousands of miles, and 140 years!

In 1997 I journeyed to Germany to meet Katja's mother Gertrud Knuth. Together with Heidi Kuglin, a cousin from New Zealand, we three women cousins from three continents traveled to the original "hometown" Polish village, a very fascinating experience. Later I received a gift from Gertrud, a drawing Katja had made of my cat Buster Kitten (page 17). That was my introduction to Katja's talent.

Over the years Katja and I have developed a wonderful friendship; she sends me files of her latest paintings and I send her my new poems. One day Katja volunteered to let me use her beautiful art in my next poetry book. *Vielen Dank*, dear cousin Katja, for this splendid and generous gift!

I hope someday soon Katja and I will be able to meet in person. There is a mutual spirit and creative energy here that connects us. And we are family.

We hope you enjoy this collaboration.

Ruth Maus
Topeka, Kansas
July 2022

POEMS

ART

The poems "Which Way To Easter Island?" and "Melancholia" were previously published online by *River City Poetry*.

That Year

Falling over a cliff slowly begins with
a single misstep, a little trip, a slight decline,
a fumble, an excuse, a denial. Nobody's falling
here. A bit off balance, some casual
resistance, grasping at a few straws, then

oh—a muttered curse, then Oh!—

gravity. A finger points

to a hazy moon, golden,
unimpressed.

Hard Pan, Daffodils

There came a time when we needed spring, when
the mud mush slops and bitter blasts pitted the
voltage of longing against the fuse of endurance.
Nobody seemed clever anymore. We
needed laughter, but how does one demand
funny? Always the Sir Authorities cranky
about mental health, telling us what by now
our penitent brains had already ossified:
that when sorrow contorts our freckled journey
there is no savor, only the leavings.

Seattle, Fall

1. Reunion
A dingy room behind a
café, metal chairs,
Formica tables, students
flocked in fine words.
Somebody reads poetry;
we all clap. I see my friend
and now the room becomes
a sonnet, with that little turn
in the final couplet.

2. Vietnamese Restaurant
The veggie roll, pale
translucent veins beneath
tight thin wrapper. Looks
like a condom, says my friend.
Tastes unfamiliar—like
turkey?—it's been so long.
A mistake says the waiter.
I'll get you another.

Melancholia

Having outlived those who loved her,
she felt the razor blade of loneliness
slice left to right on her soul, like a red
poinsettia exquisite in dark seasons,

like textured drapes smothering
the emergency exit.
Some dark suede in her core whispered
You are too sensitive, as if the hunching

of loneliness were a bladed texture
she could select like red drapes.
She hunched into the suede,
smothering the season with emergency

love from left to right.
Maybe I can outlive it, she whispered.

A Farewell To Your Reproductive Organs

To L.W.

My friend, soon there will be less of you,
those petrified, prolapsed pieces sculpted
away and passed to you in a little pickle jar
by the surgeon, tied with a red bow
for Christmas, a holiday gift of medical
precision and better than a fruitcake.

My friend, soon there will be more of you,
your sweet disposition blooming like
plumerias, filling the hollow space
where once clockworks measured time
and warmed a little bun to perfection.

My friend, if you must reflect on this
occasion, consider stamping a new tattoo
over the upcoming scar, a generous iridescent one
that says "Phooey" and let it go at that.

French Pastry

Give us this day our daily bread. Instead
the husband baked French pastry, while
the silly younger wife
considered hers an exceptionally pampered life.

One day she found the husband had been making
clandestine love to flaky men instead of baking.

There'd be no babies, swing sets, teddy bears,
no bedtime nursery rhymes. Only éclairs.
No rising to the yeasty roles of love and warm shared
        laughter,
or the lightest sugarplum of all—a happily ever after.

Years would pass before she could forgive herself the fault
of needing so much sweetness that she failed to see the salt.

Tea Time

A servile loud-mouth sirening
Hot! Hot! Hot! Hot! Hot! Hot! Hot! Or
is it a teakettle curse word set to boiling?
We concluded that cucumber

sandwiches, served with clotted cream
and Earl Grey, made the Battenburg
cakes bearable despite the earnest ladies
who served us, all over seventy with

slowly knotting hands. Each poured
her heart with every small quaint cup, but
they had been steeped too long together
in strong oolong etiquette and English folly.

High Crimes and Little Fevers*

Maybe a pair of dice, or one die, horses, slots, or sports.
A stock market playing your retirement account;
any type of health insurance, or frequently, none.
Silver spoon in mouth or famine in your land. Brakes
out of fluid, meteorites crashing, bat bites, wildfires,
holy wars, and horseshoes.

God, it's a crapshoot.

So we take our chances, play the odds, buy a ticket,
bet on a hunch, test our luck, step out on the ice,
shake dirty hands. We smoke the poison, buy
bigger guns, toss back tequila shots, strip the shelves
bare from our non-renewable and only super market.

Mostly we fiddle a feverish tarantella, white-tie-clad
puppets strangely jubilant in the surety that we've
already rolled snake eyes, when we could've bet
even money.

Which Way To Easter Island?*

It's two days—you have to want to get there—
to see the *Rapa Nui* set of stoneware,
the *moai* mega statue manifesto,
a sort of Polynesian giant floor show.

Each long-eared, fourteen-ton stone head blank-staring,
a leitmotif some might find overbearing.
Colossal cash-crop lined up like a bus stop.
You bought a mini *moai* at the gift shop,

transported it back to your native city
locked in the middle-nowhere of the prairie,
to posture on the altar by your night chest
between the Virgin Mary and an amethyst,

a rabbit's foot, a pearl, a pheasant feather,
—their mojo amplified thus grouped together.
You're hopeful their diversified behavior
will cover all the bases for a savior.

But then again this could be an endeavor
where gullibility hangs on forever.

Letter To The Administrators*

Ever since the jiggery-pokery, the landlord
owning my head has threatened eviction. So
I entered your quiet ward
for those octopus arms of healing, white birches and a
    warm halo

like a sunny constellation singing *If I Could
Shimmy Like My Sister Kate*. Please forgive me,
I think you misunderstood,
but I don't have a sister so not to be taken literally.

But now I flail flat, bottle green
and voodoo slathered sharp with devil's breath,
splayed out for the wide screen
in slow death.

My better angels piss on you for not revealing
how to love this limp sock puppet and every angry thing
    she's feeling.

Beatitudes

Blessed are the patient, for they shall be satisfied,
    eventually.

Blessed are the students, for they shall obtain mercy
    if they make half an effort.

Blessed are the weather forecasters,
    for delivering us from evil most of the time.

Blessed are those who sew the buttons back on,
    for they keep us from gapping.

Blessed are the lucky, for they always find
    a parking spot.

Blessed are the farmers, who give us
    our daily bread.

Blessed are the blacksmiths, who beat
    our swords into plowshares.

Blessed are the consumers of medical marijuana,
    for they shall see God, so I've heard.

Blessed are the poets, for theirs is the kingdom
    of all those words and occasionally
    the virtuosity to use them well.

Dedicated to…*

The woman in the hairnet and earplugs who cans pickles at the factory, dill, sweet, gherkin, kosher, chips, spears, slices, bread-and-butter pickles, and occasionally pepperoncinis, and who smells of vinegar every day as she drives home.

The lady who hordes cats, all of them disease-ridden, dirty, frightened, and reeking of ammonia, because she thinks it's about love, about saving them.

The old men, who, like cats, need love and need to keep their whiskers clean, because some say cleanliness is next to godliness.

The astronomer who searches for years to find a single new godly heaven, just a light year away from the old one.

The Star Trek fans, their bizarre costumes and weirder conventions. Live long and prosper.

The motley fools and scarecrows in their condos and corn fields.

The chemist who invented corn syrup in 1812.

The man who synchronizes stoplights, so ladies from factories won't crash driving home while listening to *Ballet Mecanique* and munching on snacks made with corn syrup.

The fallen leaves furiously dancing their *Ballet Mecanique* at The Leaf Ball, in the middle of the windy street with the synchronized stoplight, next to the pickle factory that went out of business last year, now occupied by feral cats and homeless old men.

Yum And Celebration

The Persian was penurious with her mice,
combative and injurious, to be precise.
With skill she defended her kill, now a disfigured shrine,
the mignonette morsel on which a fine feline might dine.

Some happy-go-lucky undisciplined Siamese fellow
who hadn't yet bothered to read the house-hierarchy memo,
learned at the wrong end of her claws he had better appease her,
that licking the butter left out on the counter was easier.

But a choice mouse produces the tastiest texture and crunch;
no day is complete without a mouse treat after lunch.
Worth noting: not caustic, not bloating, no bad kitty breath,
and mauling the stuffing will not induce coma or death.

All this to explain Kitty's hissing and swift scorched-earth
    ardor—
defending her claim to the alpha cat's catnip-mouse larder.

Someone's Hairy Favorites

Someone chops away your hair in the convent,
then gathers orphaned clippings off the floor
for a keepsake album in a lacquered drawer.
Hair grows back longer, meaner than before.

Someone whacks your hair in the mausoleum,
since cutting is the only remedy known
when the wools and trolls become so overgrown
they have their own time zone.

Someone shaves your head before the gallows,
the wind a stretcher-bearer of nits and pieces.
Whatever gain this brittle rite releases
the novelty of it soon ceases.

Someone cuts her own hair; but inspection
necessitates professional correction
in order not to live with furry sorrow:
horrific hair today, but gone tomorrow.

Revolution

You are
weary of revolutions, staleness
and stink
of empty beer bottles and pulpy eyes,
splinters in the lodge pole.
Too many blathers of miles of asphalt
and damn, damn, damn
the rage. But sometimes

you seek
the next revolution, praying "Push me
higher, open the wounds
and scour the debris. Throw stones
at my glass house and spray-paint
new wicked zig-zags on my
worldview."

Fall into some
black holes of misunderstanding.

You feel
sooty now –
You trampoline toward
the next misbegotten
revolution.

Grin
and bluster as you do it,
Sister,
because somehow, for the next
scrummaging interval
you have become
that revolution.

Burning the Porcupine Eggs in Ukraine

To E. M.

A mentor to get through the apocalypse
would be nice: hoard this, go there, never
use the word *democracy*.
So slow, the new normal abnormal.
No map, no shame, ever only humans
trudging after understanding and
illegal beer.

Suppose the hobgoblins won? Would
miasma be required for residency? She
tossed the sweetgum tree balls into a fire
since there was nothing else left to burn,
wishing for a marshmallow, s'mores.

Every day began at night.

Sleeping an interval; life a small clearing
in a forest of concrete. Nothing a poet
could make a crack in, or even a crumble.

Event Horizon*

Each leaf fades, falls,
contracting the universe by
one. Then another,
all. Until there remains
only a singularity.

If you ask a galaxy, it's
the head of a pin
with an angel
foxtrotting
a diminishing
offertory
i
  n
   t
    o

The Odyssey*

Serendipity University became your alma mater
when you dropped out of the overbred ivy league.
 "French verbs – *merde*!" you said.
It was time for Your Own Space Mission,
The Doors and *The Cloud of Unknowyng.*

You strayed down the right paths, exploring
sepia beaches, tea bags and hashtags, and
jewels disguised as shower curtain rings.
You never walked on water. Some days
when there was no wind for the sails,
you would play strip-Scrabble with
your stroppy friends Big Girl No. 2,
the Undertaker from Overbrook, and
Festering Turd; everybody won.

Time flowed and the planets aligned.
"Come home," you heard their Siren
voices pleading one day. "There's
no place like Kansas."

Your old front porch was prairie-hot
when you spotted your elderly parents there
sitting too still,
perhaps co-mingling with the oleander.
"Damn those Sirens," you muttered.
"I thought I was smooth, but I was not."

Then, squaring your shoulders, turned
back around and left.
"Kansas – *merde*!" was the last thing
anyone heard.

Choirboy

It's you, the former choirboy I once knew,
so long ago in some arched church somewhere.
The burden of my heart—forgiving you.

You practiced a depravity or two,
went wicked with brutality. Nowhere
the blessed former choirboy I once knew.

You've seeded sin repentance can't undo,
compounded every black deed. But beware,
I have grown weary of forgiving you.

Indulgence and the price of pain fall due.
Though luck would gift you some way to repair
the fallen former choirboy I once knew,

don't think you can escape our rendezvous.
Despite your lamentations, anguished prayer,
forgive me, but I'm not forgiving you.

But at its core this isn't about you.
As I would be forgiven, should I dare
absolve the former choirboy I once knew?
Do unto others: me forgiving you.

The Citadel

I know where the rose-colored summer goes
when it doesn't like us anymore. I know
we people-clods cement too soon,
all our black dirt insensate because
we can't expect much here in the citadel.

I know if martinets portended wealth we'd be
the stinkin' plush land of wanton soirées
and velvety polo ponies, an easy stew
of white truffles and big mythologies. But
we can't expect much here in the citadel.

If I knew you hankered for me I would
weave you a little sonnet full of dainties,
or cast you my best pigmented charm, or
stir up some silver rain. But what's an
expectation here if not a waste

or a life sentence?

February

Crisp, like the snap of a brittle cracker,
winter's wind outlines our edges,
punishing kingdoms that dismiss it too
lightly, knifing even unbelievers
and the infidels of an early spring.

A wink, then
the crocus outrageous in purples and golds,
unashamed to arrive at the party
while the host
is still cooking the feast.

Methuselah*

Old, older, oldest, full of heavy lifting, the thunderhead
of longevity.
Direct lineage of Adam so of course
the family curse. Some say
a righteous man, prophet and priest,
but I say even
the best butter will go rancid
and how wonderful can incontinence be?

Before
hip replacements
and cataract surgery, before
those badass Bingo parlors that smell
of uncleaned carpet,
there was old drooling You,
bribing each day to stretch out
time
with its curious drawer of knives.

Maybe an anomaly, but
I say we whisper Your name with envy
in our secret
and elastically foolish dreams.

July

There is nothing small about July. It is all jumbo
bleached-brilliant clouds sopping up blue broad-shouldered sky;
gluttonous picnics crammed with slap-happy family and friends who
chunk down swollen hot dogs, puffy potato salads, massive pickles,
fruity and creamy pies the size of the bowling ball juice-factory
    watermelons,
and the hand-cranked ice-packed brain-freeze vanilla ice cream
you try to leave room for.

July just revels in itself and in you, stupefied
with acres of skin showing, sunburns like wildfires; water seized
in pools, lakes, sprinklers, horse tanks, birdbaths;
birds and bunnies making baby, baby, baby. July is
a non-stop grass frenzy needing mowed, hayed, weeded; it is
dust on country roads greeting and gritting the landscape;
long easy days that slow and laze you into becoming the fatted calf.

July is big cannons booming
loud colors and percussions, sulphury symphonies fireworking
over the neighborhood, smothering summer nights as
the *oohs* and *wows* expand in testament to thunder,
overload, excess. July is a shallow grave for self-discipline,
somebody leaving you a fortune you must spend quickly.
July is a bumper-crop in your harvest of blessings.

Some Kinda Life

To be born, plop, a toot and rattle board game.
Advance five spaces, pick a card, ringworm,
relapse, or refugee. The doorbell brings shufflers,
shaggy suitors of bad smell, mostly sawdust.
Get out of jail free. Gear up, lottery tickets,
armors of plasma and fixatives, daylilies, dillydallies,
heroin. Hallelujah. Valentines for my sweet. A fever
dream: percussionist in the philharmonic
Swan Lake and *Papa's Got A Brand New Bag.*
Go directly to Coda.
Take a bow. Take two.
Plop in plot,
Marvin Gardens.

Please Refrigerate the Brie

All bruised cherries decay easily—
fragile gooseberries, highly-intoxicating juices,
kiwis, lusterless mangos, nectarines or peaches,
Quinces—react swiftly, turning unbearably
vile with xeric yesterday's zinfandel.

Soulmates

You bring your umbrella and I'll bring my crystal vase;
we'll set up house together in some gimcrackery little place,
where you can store your suitcase, where I brew a pot of tea
with hopes and hesitations and steeped leaves
    from a hazelnut tree.

You bring your religion and I'll bring my Persian cat,
perhaps a bottle of merlot and a thrift-store welcome mat.
You'll cook the spaghetti; I will play the mandolin.
Evenings will find us shiny and wearily-numb
    from the raptures of sin.

You bring your neuroses and I will bring my pain.
We'll bleed through the rough edges until
    most of those dragons are slain.
Then you'll pull out the swans, the hearts, and the galaxies
    far far away,
and I will respond with a villanelle and a calla lily bouquet.

So bring your fool's gold, Dear, and I'll bring pennies galore.
We'll have enough to rent paradise for a year and a day,
    maybe more.

The Hardest Part

You tell yourself you live a normal life,
but one day see you've played a thousand games
of spider solitaire on your device.

You realize the ones you loved have gone
with little effort or as little thought.
Perhaps it wasn't personal. You can't
demand that life will always go your way.

Dance to the expectations of the crowd.
Experience a violence or two.
Some hurt so pitiful you can't unfeel it
poisons every notion that might bring
a smile, a pleasant sentience, a joy.

So numbness make the wobbly world go 'round.

Do any of your poems tell the truth—
the hardest part defining any heart?
However sweet your sonnets, villanelles,
while holding up the looking glass it's clear
you never mention loneliness at all.

Close Relation

Flamingoes stand on one foot so they can
examine their other foot up close. This
and other natural world data, like the
fact that cats, although musical, never form
a jazz ensemble, presumes a curiosity
not always present in humans.

But if you're interested I will tell you
a male platypus produces venom
during mating season.

Self-Portrait

You drew deep

shadows and reflecting light,
lines and curves, perspective, texture. Hours
then days spent.

copying the familiar portrait
visited by millions. Intricate tiny waves
in the long borrowed hair, embroidered bodice
and puffy sleeves, the plump hands
folded neatly over themselves in the lap
just so.

But

with a hand mirror to your face
you drew your own precise visage, layered your own
anomalous smirk and gaze onto the
half-hammy painting.
One a lady and one a poignant parody, contrarily,
and much more

than you intended to reveal.

Order

There's safety in good habits. Tidy,
solid, set routines are best.
Laundry, sweep, and mop each Friday,
towels and sheets exactly pressed.

Socks by color in the sock drawer.
Shoes by season on shoe trees;
boots lined up on closet's clean floor,
purposefully and with ease.

Books arranged by topic and size.
Canned goods stacked a certain way.
Diligent and organized,
though why so careful I can't say.

Filing each form in its right place,
folders alphabetically.
Being neat is no disgrace
and I make no apology.

I survey the prim results
obsessively, despite the day
when you with one grand feckless insult,
died in bloody disarray.

So the sun will still come up,
the rain will fall, the orchards bloom.
But I must fill the peppermill
and dust the goddamned dining room.

In the Back Yard, Part I

Pretty Bird

I've cocked my eye on you, pretty bird, both of us
back in the back yard, greedy for the end of false spring
with its buttermilk-paint chill.

For your nursery you've selected the same hedgerow
as previous years,
still wall-papered in wild rose brambles
and deadly thorns. This hospitable spring/summer condo
provides a safe roost for numerous lodgers
while growing its own rain-shedding intertwined overhangs.
On the ground floor the occasional indulgent rabbit
darts amidst the canes, your *hopalong* doorman.

Softening ground confers the nest-building-supply store,
disarranged bits of broken twigs, stalk straws, scraps
of fence-trapped miscellany, all felled and imported
by March's thoughtful winds.

My landlord duties require filling many mossy birdbaths
because your dozens of avian cousins arrive with demands.
They crowd and splash non-stop, unblushingly
like water is free, theirs for the unmetered taking, theirs
to moisten feathers and so set tender eggs
with optimal humidity.

I have foresworn using chemicals on the soil, the part
of your restaurant under my safekeeping. Instead
I sow clover between the dandelions, tiny specks
of mini-dwarf seed ordered from a catalog. Bees
will come to clover, bees to pollenate the purple
Echinacea and gold Rudbeckia, jewel-like
adornments that will awaken soon from their
seasonal dreams.

For a long moment, pretty bird, you and I
acknowledge each other in an unspoken pact.
We will both
brave the new nursling world with intention, clacking
and winking as this shamelessly giddy season unfolds—
nature's midges and spores and hatchlings—
so promising,
so pretty.

In the Back Yard, Part II

Three Bunnies

I found the rabbit nest by accident,
and fearing mom would then abandon it,
marked nest with stakes and string and so bestowed
assurance that the nest would not get mowed.

Emerging bunnies now possess my yard;
I call them Clytemnestra, Pearl, Bernard.
They shred my lilies when they're in the mood.
They nosh my hostas as a favorite food.
They double-joint a carom sideways hop
then launch straight up—like watching popcorn pop.

There's something nursery rhyme in all of this
too anthropomorphic to dismiss.
As I, the landlord, presumed *force majeure*,
absorb these fancies as eager voyeur
and too familiar fairy godmother.

In the Back Yard, Part III

Happy

It is a day for bench-sitting, becoming the slice of this moment,
sniffing the glue that binds then releases us, recycles and
repeats us.

It is a day the happy is too strong,
petunias carelessly flashing their pinks wild to the world.

A backyard squirrel *knows*, then gnaws a beautiful walnut,
bracketed in the parentheses of approaching autumn. Two
small lizards skip through the potted palms and succulents,
nowhere else they would rather be, an all-expense-paid
life requiring a few bugs and the ability to fold in on oneself,
some patchwork sun.

There is breadth in happy here, just breathing, sprawling its way
through the puddings and capillaries, stretching and stretching,
bigger than a carpenter's rule or the square root of *pi*. Bigger
than me.

I have captured happy and will eat it for breakfast tomorrow
and I will eat it every day after that.

The Courtship On The 40th Floor

To A. K.

I wear my Grandmother Esther's pink necklace
and spot the Statue of Liberty out the window.
You in your baggy Calvin Klein suit
—a New Yahwk lahyer coaxing some
innocuous prairie species of womankind.
So far, a prairie chicken.

Your office on the 40th floor—and you
afraid of heights. In Kansas no silo
rears quite so high. Across the desk
in the corporate tower we stare like adversaries,
city-tillers of hot bodies and cool persuasions,
trembling.

You point out landmarks, the Chrysler Building,
museums. What would Esther have made of this?
I fight the urge to flee, though I'm not afraid
of heights.

The sign in the office kitchenette says
"Healing In Progress." That there should be
such wisdom amidst the confidential tax files
of rock stars and presidents reassures me—
a gift flourishing at this altitude!

So hear my hesitation for the Kansas wheat it is:
golden and heavy-with-heart, needing to be ready,
mature, tall.

Maybe even as high as the 40th floor.

Indenture

Most words roll around content in their downy identity,
a good scratch on the dazzle parts, the warts, the equipoise
and all those innuendoes. You hear how they love themselves;
you get it. So as you hang out together at pre-school you babble
and bond. You whisper and snort with them under your breath
at the doctor's office. You take them and their boozy curses
out to the ole' ball game. You choke them back at funerals.
These Old Friends imprint in your vocabulary, stored
in your mental address book until you call on them for
oration, like dialing up a hot date, confident, smooth-like.

Some words shy away. They avoid you, they act invisible
like a word in a Witness Protection Program. There's *kern,*
a light-armed Irish foot soldier now masquerading
as a print shop helper. And *throve,* an antiquarian holed up
in the dictionary's dilapidated boarding house who
comes out once a year for meals, blinded by the light.
Secrets. Troubled pasts. Obsolete icons. You can snicker,
but these uneasy words have shape-shifted and morphed
noun to verb or worse, trying to fit a flat former life
onto a now circular plane without being spotted
by etymologists and cunning crossword enthusiasts.

Eventually a word wrinkles, ceases all the utility or pleasure
it once embodied. *What shall we do with it?* someone asks,
this old word that no one comes to visit. Quietly it is evicted
from the boarding house, its little or long life severed
and forgotten, left alone to die of starvation. Whole families
of words, unlucky archaic languages, sometimes suffer
this forsakening.

If you turn over enough rocks you may spot dried alien carcasses like *prognathous* or *scorbutic*; you will not recognize them as words. But knowing that once there was a time when they molded themselves in indenture to us, reified a snippet of our vigor and anger, our descriptions, wit, and love, we will salute them, disconnectedly, as one salutes the ancestors.

Future-Perfect

Come, let us stumble to that lush park
sometime before dawn, but after dark,
to make our way through all the fens and ferns of doubtful meaning,
to clutch at nearness during quarantining.

Your protests scatter on the wind like dry geraniums and notes
whispered once in future-perfect quotes,
whose yellowed ashes evidence our atrophied connection
lurching, I am sure, in the wrong direction.

As streetlamps press long shadows on the velvet-tangled green,
we flicker gently, quietly, obscene,
unaccustomed to all the buttons and trumpets of such dangerous debris
that I exchange in the park at night with you and you with me.

Airbrushed*

Hello, I'm Julie and welcome to my blog, she writes
in the way young people do trying to find themselves.
She's grown out of the measles-and-oatmeal stage,
survived enough English classes to still love language,
and seems keen that her messy, meaningful words
should be cast upon the metaverse waters.
Look at me,
I am so sensitive, showing you my silkiest feelings.
She posts the delicate poems she's written, sharing
comments about life, what she thinks of as life.

Somewhere an intense young swain stumbles through
his high school play rehearsal. Still channeling
a romantic in his ridiculous foul-smelling doublet,
he surfs Julie's website, smitten by a screen.
Prithee, he thinks, *canst this be my Juliet, my sun?*
He responds in his best Shakespeare imitation,
a modern wooing in old oratory.

God, I used to write that stuff.
Ethereal whimsies and watercolors washes,
over-sized yearnings puffed with pain
and swollen by the pollen of desire that floated
everywhere in my air then. Before hard knocks
and pursuit of easy-money set in, blah, blah, blah.
But you've had your own broken hearts, crushed egos
that showed no mercy, never mind
the self-medications that we won't go into.

The airbrush of reality has deleted most of those
youthful longings from me,
because innocence only freshens in one direction.
Still, as The Bard himself once said,
How far that little candle throws its beams.
I am rooting for you, Julie.

Infrared

Cabal plots and superstitions,
mother-church of all munitions.
Contraband, concealed carry,
neutralize the adversary.
One-way trip to mortuary.

Each selects our claw and cluster,
nuclear to knuckle-duster,
toxic round obscene and sour,
frenzied blood lust firepower.
Growing redder by the hour.

Losing ground with rubefaction,
ruinous in thought and action.
Ever meaner our fixation
chum-feeding a wet-red nation.
Father, hear our supplication.

Primrose path to Armageddon,
close to death, but far from Heaven.

Coach

Who runs the draft and sends us in the game?
(Life or game the same and most don't care.)
Who whacks our butts, while we exhale a prayer?
Please let my time be worthy of acclaim.

The snap: a jolt of bulky aberrations.
We fumble as they slam us like a truck
and can't recover. Maybe just our luck,
or maybe our neurotic expectations.

We need someone to blame for all the maddening
impersonal yet personal attacks
severe enough to stop us in our tracks,
as well as for (ahem) the extra padding.

We bounce and boogie to the marching band,
forgetting there will be a final score.
Who failed to diagram all this before?
Who let this Game of Life get out of hand?

Puzzled

She stuffed disparate pieces into
the jigsaw puzzle of her life,
seldom gracefully,
here a fender-bender, there a fer-de-lance,
a handful of stupendous blessings.
Occasionally she stepped back, puzzled,
to view the result. Hard to say—
Impressionist? Surreal?

Once she considered what would happen if,
at the end, a single piece were missing,
as if an inconsequential cat had hockey-pucked it
to the floor and under the karmic sofa
so that the path out of the garden
would never become her road
to enlightenment.

She sighed and harrumphed at
the crazy colors,
awkward shapes,
and uneven energies
that had kaleidoscoped themselves
into such a brave assembly.
She knew then they would always
remain a puzzle.

Organ Donor

You gotta love a carcass,
rich, fermented, puffy and unselfish,
welcoming all, favoring none.

You gotta tempt the patrons,
confections to snarl over,
savor. All-you-can-eat and free.
Peckers and bone pickers,
bacteria and beetles sashay to the table,
a little place setting for each.
Leftovers for take-out,
femur-lickin' good
and no tip jar.

You gotta face the drama
with the Manna.
Everybody scheduled to be the buffet,
welcoming all, favoring none.

Sleep

I.

Dust ruffles in the pseudo womb
we fluff, starch, decorate;
slack bodies parallel
a waffle-ironed counter weight.

II.

A-man-about-a-dog dream,
the road-kill of brain's debris,
ignoring a bladder one bark away
from a wet warm wee.

III.

Unconscious but *somewhere,* we marinate
in marrowbones and chords,
an undressed rehearsal
of the sleep we're moving towards.

Yowl

Can we yowl together? Can we blast this bolt-
hole lament? Never mind the acoustic properties;
never doubt your vocal range, your plastic-y pitch—
yowl is not a harmonic. Yowl so

as not to heed the dissonance all-surrounding,
the scabrous whore of war, as filthy
and nimble as a tubercular bacchanal, some
Gordian knot never untangling and all

the bleached wood crosses dovetailed
nicely, but none feather-light. God, yes,
we will now
yowl.

Pandemic in The Time of Roses

I.

My favorites are the pink ones,
each delicate as a
china teacup. Inevitably
they surrender, crumbling
like desiccated wallpaper.

II.

Protective masks, ignored by the masses
during summer's fevers. A solitary bee
ignores masses of blooms, circling instead
to the roses.
A breeze sniffs through the garden
stalking her, stalking us.

III.

Today marks my father's birthday,
in June, the time of roses.
Masks plead for purchase,
blooming everywhere
with landscaped prints, team logos, the
inevitable skull-and-crossbones.
My favorites are the pink ones.

IV.

Roses protect the summer's graves,
delicate as china teacups.

All the Sly Horses

She's back in the saddle for another ride,
clutching, uncertain, and terrified.
Despite her splendid distrust of men
starting over again.

It's not quite as simple as she thought it would be—
flirtation, like muscle, can atrophy.
Though she dolls up, mounts up, to play along,
new men, like sly horses, are snorting, headstrong.

Just as it seems like needless war
and all her parts are saddle-sore,
she gathers herself, a feminine flower
recalling she has inherent power,

that even when twitchiness can't be denied
there's nothing as fun as the thrill of the ride.
Let her mount take the bit in his teeth—she will stay.
Leave walking for another day.

Parent

She blamed their disquieting fathers—English
classes, emotive poets, an engorged dictionary—
so the kids just kept on popping out.
Most were unremarkable. Others she barely recognized.
Some so hideous they could only be drowned at birth.

Many years she nursed them, allowing them
to become and say what they wanted to be.
Every family has its outliers. Hers chose the forms
of elegies and sonnets, silliness and slam, each
tripping and slobbering over itself to get to the page.

What does a parent do with *mucho* sparrow-legged
frock-coated progeny? Love them the best you can;
claim them like the popinjay you are;
and hope that perhaps
one or two will light up the world.

Hey You

Make hay while the sun shines.
                    —Traditional saying.

Mow hay while it is green,
about 12 to16 inches tall, but before it flowers.
Hay cut and raked into windrows requires

three days curing in the sun

before it can be safely baled. Morning dew
will add back moisture. Hay above 15% moisture
can smolder for months inside a bale or a barn,

then ignite. Oh no! Bales should be densely packed.

Get off the tractor and kick them to check this;
your foot should smart just a little.
Hay inside the bale should be bright green.

Moldy hay, grey or black, is bad hay.

Don't buy it and don't feed it to your livestock,
as it will cause colic, respiratory conditions,
and other bilious quandaries.

Haying begins around Memorial Day.

Sometimes you can grow three cuttings' worth
in one season. Sometimes Mother Nature ruins it all.
Put a Slow Moving Vehicle sign

on the back of your trailer.

Freshly cut hay, especially alfalfa, smells
sweet, caramelized, a little like maple syrup.
You and the man lying in the hayloft's

mounds of loose hay, watching cupola pigeons above.

Hay is scratchy. He was muscular, smooth.
Now in his absence, there is no sun; you cannot
make hay. It smarts, just a little.

Sometimes Grass

speaks to you.

Listen.
Hear how it grows, green or brown-bladed from
earth
or maybe from some crack crying in a sad sidewalk,
semi-sentient
to be ripped, chewed, poisoned, mutilated
by munching monsters,
machines shrieking death-to-you-in-my-sights, Grass;
crippled
by careless crews of professional lawn dudes.

Feel
Grass on skin; lay prostrate, stroking textures
tickle,
stalks and edges, leaves and heads
purring restless components
of baskets, nests, shrouds woven from
Grass bodies,
Grass ghosts murmuring *useful purpose*.

It
doesn't have to be one-sided.
Talk to Grass. Tell Grass
you know that rippling in breeze, smelling
sweet and keeping score,
its stealth runners, seeds,
gobble
all that openness, spreading, invading.
And how out of sympathy and
spite,
because *it's always greener in your neighbor's yard*,
you just smile.

Storm Trooper

Stiff phalanxes. Police in riot gear, tight rows six-seven deep
holding the line against protesters at night on the downtown street.

Black-clad, these Darth Vaders, armed and bullhorning *Halt! Obey!*
as a single protester, hands raised in surrender, offers up a pink
    bouquet.

Could you be such a person, so brave against the odds?
Or would you hate those dark-clad warriors doing their jobs?

Would you stand-down to accept that soft gift if you were a Darth?
Just remember, big Storm Trooper, that the meek shall inherit the
    Earth.

Avatar

They look so at ease ambling left to right on my
screen, some right to left, no matter. Many
wade or surf. Others recline in real time under
flapping canvas umbrellas, or meditate on a

towel. Live webcam scenes only 3,000 miles
and one paradise away. We all find our own
antivenom to the endless mean months
of permafrost north. I see

the yellow flag is out. Palm trees wave to me.
Fuchsia bougainvillea, turquoise ocean, white sand.
Is it really *that* simple? Everybody barefoot,
swim suits, shorts and baggy tees. Watching

those fools abusing their tender skins, don't
they know that when they shed their pin stripes
they became *my* hirelings, avatars deconstructing
my frigid dolor? Each pixel a palpable

grace. If a sea anemone were to whisper my name
I would renounce everything.

Strategies For Shame

The tomatoes begin blushing,
embarrassed at their vulnerable nakedness, swollen
bellies of pulp and seed. Green grows to rust, then
orange, finally flame, as heat and time
and inevitability
bring them flushed and around
to our way of eating.

Embarrassed cats, incapable of blushing's
red reveal, suddenly lickity-lickity
grooming themselves. *You see*, the cat
performs her shtick, *this was my purest intention
all along.* Such slight-of-paw distraction
paints the cat's coat and conscience in assuagement,
until inevitably no blemish remains.

You begin blushing,
embarrassed at your vulnerable everything,
pulpy ego swollen, belly of inferiority.
Inflamed you grow to guilt, then
grief, finally fading as inevitably
the seeding of your dust compels
our compassion.

Stupid Season*

When Peter Sellers says to Shirley MacLaine, *"Shall we gather the apricots together at my farm in Méjean, Paulette?"* was he seducing a beautiful widow at her husband's funeral, or seeking unpaid help for the harvest? These

    are the questions driving you to seek answers
    from sticky buns at three in the morning, straining to break into
    the code-breakers club,
    about a parsec too cerebral for most.

    When The School of Wisecrack Puns and Outrageous Retorts
    expels you, is it because
    you didn't scatter the ashes as instructed, or because you
        inscribed

    "The Cheese Stands Alone" on the tombstone? After
    all, venom and gastropods should mix well, if only
    when they mate during Stupid Season and
    it's always time to fall in love again, to look at the other

    and see wounds still unhealed. Don't you always dance for the
        apricots?
    Surrender, therefore, to the Season and disport yourselves
    with all those indigestible and grossly sticky buns.

Influencer

You are the shift key that changes everything
on our keyboard, the herald even the angels
hark to. You dispense duplicity electronically,
throwing the baby out with the nonchalance while
modeling flash. Money, merit,

mousetrapping the malleable minds of disciples
who click Like and subscribe jonesing
Please, half-naked god, give us this day our
next big juicy apple.
How can it be that this god is so zippy, then

withers so unskillfully that even the angels cringe
and the keyboard enters a newer name?

Hollow

So we huddled under shelves, inside caves
with air conditioning, pretending we weren't
choosing our die-off and decay, decay as

leafy verdants seared, yellowed, katydids
didn't, glaciers stammered away, away. That
frantic conservation—so passé. Officials

groomed their hollow heads and led us
further astray, astray, bleached in denial as
we jet-fueled to snappy Rome

or maybe the burlesque of Pompeii.
Have you anticipated how this ends,
one preventable day, that ignoble day?

Would we act to heal our planet without
delay, delay? But a bluebird discerned
from its soured home and restlessly chirruped

"Not with a bang, but a *tu-a-wee*.
Make way. Make way."

Meditation

Calm down the slog even further, almost
to dazed, then decide if the day
will digest. Some are all calendars
and breadcrumbs, capacities
or deformities, so you develop
strategies and gather your tools

for confronting the obvious.
Not the best, obviously, but
still getting the focus in focus
by

clearing the energies and storing
the quibbles for a later
venue.

The Art Museum

Here a Pollock, there a parchment, everywhere a pigment.
It's a climate-controlled cave where you pay
to confirm your cultural ignorance
and call it entertainment.

Egyptian temples and soup can labels,
Art Nouveau, Caravaggio,
Noguchi, Picasso, de Kooning, and Rothko,
Klimt, and Kandinski, O'Keefe, and Da Vinci,
Savage, Cassatt, Kahlo, Basquiat. What's the meaning of what we're looking at?
Wood cuts, totems, Mona, and Lichenstein;
each one unique in period, purpose, medium, style, and design.
You pretend to study them all: Raphael, Hockney, Munch, Vermeer, Chagall,
portraits like Whistler's Mama, lots of gruesome religious drama,
landscapes, abstracts, sculpture, jewelry, figures in clay.
This could take all day.
Porcelains, glassware, tribal masks, and photographs,
plundered ancient icons in gold, and the old
marble statues,
anatomically correct, that you like very much.

DON'T TOUCH

In the heady throes of art afterglow
the Gift Shop sells silk scarves and posters,
paperweights, and coasters so you can take a little piece
of Van Gogh back to Paxico, though they also have irises
and starry nights among that hamlet's local sights.
But art? Nothing springs to mind.
Or at least not like *that* kind.

Great Expectations

Uncle Manfred never spent a lot.
But then, we only saw him twice a year.
Saved every honest cent he ever got—
some say stingy; he preferred austere.

This shy man never thought to take a wife,
or move to town or go beyond eighth grade.
Just farmed the family homestead all his life
and planned to take his fortune to the grave.

Then at eighty-four his wish prevailed,
when Uncle Manfred left for paradise.
We gasped when the gold casket was unveiled;
two hundred thousand dollars was its price.

The Will was read; then grief intensified.
but sadly, not because the man had died.

Scar

In the little curio shop located deep
in The Valley of Pain, a holy place
peddling odd icons and alternate
realities,
you picked up the scar and brought it home.

From that day on you and your scar were
inseparable.
You filtered life through the young scar,
bent to its demands, protected it from
all things inflammatory. You wore it

like a combat medal pinned
on skin
and psyche, the graffiti
of biology, the logo of survival.
One day when your mind was clear

you inhaled beyond *I am wounded*—
the scar you had labeled unlovely
had infused you its effortless glitter,
waiting for you to recognize
it had been a star all along.

The Memory

The memory lies dormant in your head,
languishing in muscle, cell, and bone—
softly, so as not to wake the dead.

A trigger starts a trickle. Then, well-fed,
the smallest thought reveals an undertone,
cracks the former sureness of your head.

Leaking feelings from which you have fled,
resurrecting tender parts, you moan,
softly, so as not to wake the dead.

Once unbound the memory will spread—
despite the willful ignorance you've shown
nothing can stay dormant in your head.

Face to face with awful things you dread,
is there any horror you can't disown?
Any shelter once you wake the dead?

Better to behead the beast instead:
chain it, cage it, kill it to postpone
the reckoning of memory in your head.
Let the dead lie softly, surely dead.

Barbels

When you were a minnow
I was a mallard paddling like hell,
eating you for lunch because
I could. But
the pond was darkled
and you escaped.

When you were a loach
I admired your barbels, *what
diminutive whiskers you have,*
said Goldilocks. You
lived on the bottom, out of
my reach.

When you were a piranha
I thrashed the other way,
afraid you would
scarify my flesh, worse,
just as I once tried to lay hold of you;
the food chain; the power.

Life Is Full of Disappointments

Your ice cream scoop falls off the cone,
Your golden lab chokes on a bone.
It rains on your long-planned parade
Just lemons—never lemonade.
The microwave burns down your house.
The neighbor runs off with your spouse.
Your Tesla and your stocks both crash.
Your Facebook friends are talkin' trash.
Your teen-ager consumes your stash.
You get a poison ivy rash.
Your banker says you're out of cash.
Enough to make your teeth ga-nash.

At times like this, turn to a pro:
as Buddha said, "Let that shit go."

Empire

The recluse slides into his own empire, effecting
hallowed halls
out of airless walls, proclaiming commandments
from snake-bit habits. He is a hole in the wind,
his moat, figurative and figment-thin,
sparing him the unlearned fops
and smarty deal-makers who would
squeeze his entrails.

He is not a little bit celestial. No
divine-right altar call or prayer shawl,
only straining anxiety through lace curtains.
Sliding, slacking, finally the hardened hole
in his own wind, the lost latitude
of Mondo Solitude.
Where else would he go all alone,
if not to his greasy Lazy-boy throne?

The Words

Part I

The Words have flat-lined, refusing to speak to you,
not even a hex or maladroit curse.
Perhaps you didn't wordsmith the architecture of their nature.
Possibly the tortured ones wanted showcased with big drama
and high horror and the rough-and-tumble ones needed coddled.
Maybe you stacked them too stiffly, coughing
when you should have stroked, murmured.
Still their ghostly and gooey and gap-toothed cosmology
feels weighty to you, the dazzle-factor of royalty
counting fat chests of jewels.
So you beg as one would to an altar god:
feed me your voice again,
desperate for the tickle and fizz
that only comes from
their champagne.

The Words

Part II

They swarm you like gnats, buzzing and pestering
to gain a toe-hold in your consciousness,
clouds of words
straining secretions of persistence,
needing your craft as their crutches, craving corpulence.
Galloping and slinking, coasting and stinging they
come, cognating and fuddling, faulting and clotting,
blazing and praising and obfuscating your ratty
resistance with their red mullet and dragon demands.
One does an arabesque, tin tiddling. Another
cartwheels badly, a lumpy potato. But
Praise The Lord, occasionally and without effort, sometimes
they sing.

The Words

Part III   The Last Word on Poetry

To write like Tom Elliott,
one first must excel at it,
bending, coercing
the structure of versing.
Ah, poetry. Those
who would dare to compose
must touch the sublime.
Well, I try—all the time.

Somedays it sounds right—
almost, but not quite.
The meter's not true
and the words fly askew,
complex or cliché,
a complete disarray.
The fat lady sang,
just a whimper, no bang.

But once in a while,
when The Wordsmith Gods smile,
the words will assemble
to make the earth tremble.
No waste land. Behold—
a rare poem, all gold.
Poetry will transcend,
the beginning.

The End.

Notes*

High Crimes and Little Fevers: *Little Fever* is a slang term for rolling a five in the game of craps. *Snake eyes* is rolling a single pip on each of two dice, associated with a snake's treachery and betrayal.

Which Way To Easter Island?: The *Rapa Nui* are the aboriginal Polynesian inhabitants of Easter Island in the Pacific Ocean. *Moai* (meaning "statue" in *Rapa Nui*) are giant monolithic human figures carved from volcanic ash between 1250 and 1500.

Letter To the Administrators: "I Wish I Could Shimmy Like My Sister Kate" is an up-tempo jazz dance song written by Armand J. Piron and published in 1922.

Dedicated To: George Antheil's *Ballet Mécanique* is a musical percussion work that debuted in Paris in 1926. Sponsored by an American patroness, at the end of the concert she was tossed in a blanket by three baronesses and a duke. The work enraged some of the concert-goers.

Event Horizon: The *event horizon* is the boundary defining the region of space around a black hole from which nothing (not even light) can escape.

The Odyssey: The original "Odyssey" is an epic Greek poem written around the 8th or 7th century BCE depicting the 20-year journey of Odysseus, king of Ithaca, and the perils he encountered after the Trojan War. Themes include return, wandering, guest-friendship, testing, and omens.

The Doors were a controversial and influential 1960's counterculture rock band, the first American band with eight consecutive gold LPs selling over 100 million records worldwide. The band took its name from the title of Aldous Huxley's book *The Doors of Perception*, itself a reference to a quote by William Blake.

The Cloude of Unknowyng is an anonymous work of Christian mysticism written in Middle English in the latter half of the 14th century. It suggests that the way to know God is to abandon consideration of God's activities and attributes and be courageous enough to surrender one's mind and ego to the realm of "unknowing", at which point one may begin to glimpse the nature of God.

Methuselah: The human who lived the longest of all figures mentioned in the Bible, supposedly 969 years. His named is used as a metaphor for longevity.

Airbrushed: The Shakespeare quote is from *The Merchant of Venice*.

Stupid Season: Last line of the movie *Woman Times Seven (Sette volte donna)* a 1967 Italian/French/American comedy-drama consisting of seven episodes mostly dealing with adultery.

About the Author

Ruth Maus, a native of Topeka, Kansas, has followed a love of learning around the world to places large and small, to pyramids and hedgerows, presidential balls and Kansas hayfields.

She represented Smith College at the annual Glasscock Intercollegiate Poetry Contest where past contestants have included James Merrill, Sylvia Plath, Katha Pollit, Mary Jo Salter, James Agee, Frederick Buechner, Kenneth Koch, Donald Hall, William Manchester, Muriel Rukeyser, and Gjertrud Schnackenberg. Her poems have appeared in a variety of literary publications.

Her first book of poetry, *Valentine*, published by Meadowlark Press, was a finalist in the 2019 Birdy Contest.

In her own words:

> "I am delighted and humbled that Katja so generously offered me her beautiful artwork to enhance this book. She is so talented and I know this is a gift from the heart. Thank you dear cousin Katja!"

Photograph by Bill Stephens

About the Artist

Katja Weiss, a native of Kiel, Germany, has always been attracted to art. After completing her education she spent one year in St. Louis, Missouri, as an *au pair* and perfected her English. The "wonderful and eventful time in the States" had a huge influence on her life.

Back in Germany she developed her artistic style over the years and now specializes in oil painting. She especially loves to paint the beautiful seascapes, wide views and vast beaches of Northern Germany and nearby Denmark where she and her family spend a lot of time. She lives near Hamburg, Germany, with her husband and grown daughter.

In her own words:

"As a small child I always wanted to become a professional artist. I could see myself standing in a big studio, surrounded by colors, paint-brushes and canvasses, painting all day long.

"Although I have not become a professional artist, I never lost the passion for it and still love to paint. In fact, whenever I have time I am in the mood for it—I dive into the world of art. For me it is the best way of expressing myself, taking a break from my daily routine and staying sane. In addition I work in the prestigious Hamburger Kunsthalle, one of the most popular art museums in Germany, surrounded by historical, classical and contemporary art. What a wonderful combination!

"A painting lasts forever, is linked to emotions and memories. You can get lost in a painting or you can simply hang it up for decoration. It's all up to you.

"I am very happy to be part of this beautiful book and look forward to meeting Ruth in person one day.

"Do not hesitate to contact me if you have any questions about my paintings. I am happy to hear from you via email at katja_weiss@gmx.de. You can also see more paintings on my website www.katjaspaintings.de — welcome to my world."

Photograph provided by Katja Weiss

Meadowlark POETRY

Books are a way to explore, connect, and discover. Poetry incites us to observe and think in new ways, bridging our understanding of the world with our artistic need to interact with, shape, and share it with others.

Publishing poetry is our way of saying—

We love these words,
we want to preserve them,
we want to play a role in sharing them
with the world.

Meadowlark Press
— since 2014 —

meadowlarkpoetrypress.com

"Wry and rue---it sounds like the recipe for a craft cocktail. But those are really the main ingredients in Ruth Maus's sly wise and expansive book . . . Most of her poems are short—and a lot bigger than they seem, poems marked by gallows humor and a poker face, and with just a twitch of a tell that reveals how much lies beneath their surface."

Michael Gorra, author of *Portrait of a Novel: Henry James and the Making of an American Masterpiece*

"Witty and contemporary, Maus's poems are an energetic delight. She seems to blend the magic of the folk tale with the cutting crackle and static of modern life. The results are like blasts from the radio, when you turn the dial— each unique, each with something different to say."

Kevin Rabas, author of *Like Buddha-Calm Bird*, Poet Laureate of Kansas, 2017-2019

meadowlarkpoetrypress.com

www.ingramcontent.com/pod-product-compliance
Lightning Source LLC
Chambersburg PA
CBHW040855120626
46551CB00001B/30